Where Are the WHALES?

By Suzanne Weyn

Liz and Jon are in Australia with their parents for nine months. The children miss their friends back home in the United States. Read this book to learn how Liz and Jon share one of their adventures with their friends.

Contents

Chapter 1

A Surprise Trip

Liz and Jon Scott were far from home. They had come to Australia with their parents.

Liz and Jon were twins. Both of them were in the third grade. The Scotts were staying in Australia for nine months. Mr. and Mrs. Scott were working at a **university**.

The twins liked Australia. They knew their parents liked working at the **university**. Yet Liz and Jon missed their friends at home. They wrote to them by e-mail every day.

One night at dinner, Mr. Scott **announced** some exciting plans. “We’re taking a trip this weekend. We’ll go out on a special boat. We’ll be able to see some whales.”

“Can we take pictures of the whales?” Liz asked. “Maybe we can e-mail them to our friends at home. They’re studying whales right now.”

“Let’s bring the video camera,” Mrs. Scott said. “Then you can make a video of the whales.”

“That’s a great idea!” said Jon.

Jon and Liz e-mailed their friends at home. They **announced** that very soon they would be sending them a video of real whales.

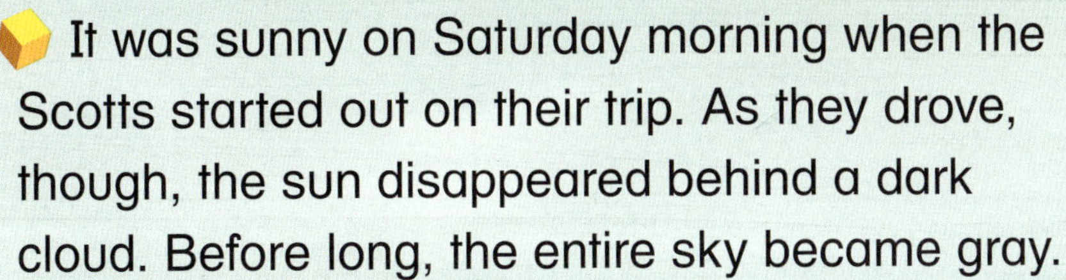

It was sunny on Saturday morning when the Scotts started out on their trip. As they drove, though, the sun disappeared behind a dark cloud. Before long, the entire sky became gray.

A drop of rain hit the car window. Then another fell. Mr. Scott switched on the wipers. "Don't worry," he said. "The weather report said to expect a nice weekend."

After driving for several hours, the family stopped at a lighthouse on the coast. "Let's get out of the car and take a look," said Mr. Scott.

"Where is it?" Jon asked. "I can't see anything."

"It's there," Mrs. Scott said. "It's hard to see because of the rain."

"Maybe we should forget whale watching today. We can go on Sunday. Let's go to a movie instead," said Mr. Scott.

Chapter 2

Everyone Wants Whales

After seeing the movie, the Scotts arrived at the hotel where they were staying. Jon and Liz checked their e-mails. They wanted to see if anyone had replied to them.

Jon counted 25 e-mail messages from their friends. "Look how many e-mails we got," Jon said. "Our friends are excited about seeing our whale video."

Liz read the e-mail messages. The twins' friends had told their teacher about the video. "Our teacher is going to show the video to the whole class. They need it by next Wednesday," Liz said.

"We'd better make sure it's good," Jon said.

"What kind of whales will we see tomorrow?" Liz asked.

"We'll be looking for humpback whales," their father answered.

"They are fun to watch because they throw their bodies up out of the water. That's called breaching. The humpbacks are **migrating** north at this time of year," said Mrs. Scott.

"Well, I sure hope they will be **migrating** while we're on the boat," Jon said. "I just got a new e-mail. Now the whole school is going to see our whale video!"

"You sound nervous about that," Mrs. Scott observed.

"I am," Jon admitted. "What if we don't see a single whale?"

"Don't worry. We should be able to catch sight of lots of whales," Mr. Scott said. "This is the time of year when both female and male whales migrate. They travel in large groups."

"Did you know that whales sing?" Mrs. Scott asked Liz and Jon.

"You're kidding," answered Liz.

"No, it's true," said Mrs. Scott. "Both female and male whales make calls. The male's calls sound like songs. The males do most of the singing. They sing to find other whales. They also sing to attract female whales."

"I wish we could hear them," Liz said.

"You would have to be under water to hear them," Mr. Scott said. "I once heard a recording of whale songs. They sound pretty amazing."

Chapter 3

Fog...Fog...Everywhere

Jon and Liz woke up early on Sunday. Liz drew back the hotel curtain. "Where did everything go?" Jon cried in alarm.

All the twins could see was a thick blanket of grayish **fog**. "This is our last day here. Does this mean we won't see any whales at all?" Liz asked. "What about our video? Everyone back home is expecting it!"

Mr. Scott looked out. "The **fog** might clear up," he said. They ate breakfast and then got in the car. They drove to a large dock. On the dock was a company that ran whale-watching tours for visitors.

The sign in front of the company's office read: CLOSED TODAY BECAUSE OF FOG. Everyone got back in the car. Mr. Scott drove to two more places. But they were also closed because of the fog.

"We'll have to come back another time. You can make your film another day," Mrs. Scott said as they stood on a dock.

"The teacher invited the whole school to watch the video just four days from now," Liz said.

Just then, Liz and Jon saw a man and a woman walking toward them. Mr. Scott's face broke into a big smile. "Wait right here," he told his family.

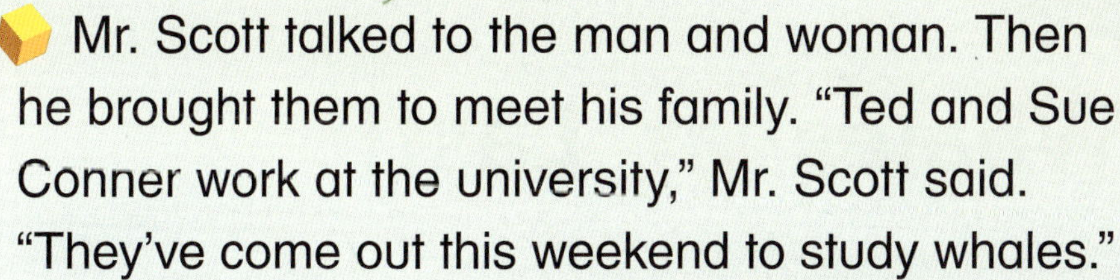

Mr. Scott talked to the man and woman. Then he brought them to meet his family. “Ted and Sue Conner work at the university,” Mr. Scott said. “They’ve come out this weekend to study whales.”

“I guess you’re not going to be able to see any whales either,” said Liz.

“No, we’re going out now. The university has its own boat here,” Ted replied. “We think it is safe to go out now. The weather is clearing up. Would you like to come with us?”

“Yes!” Liz and Jon both cried out.

Chapter 4

Whales at Last!

Before the boat had gone very far, the sun started peeking through the clouds. "I told you the weather would be fine," said Ted.

"What **research** are you doing out here today?" Mrs. Scott asked Ted and Sue.

"We hope to record the songs of the humpback whale," Sue answered. "New **research** shows that whales make more sounds than we once thought they did. We want to find out what some of those sounds mean."

"What could they be saying?" Jon asked.

"We think that sometimes they might be giving directions to other whales or expressing anger," Sue said. "Other times, they might just be giving a friendly greeting to one another."

Liz noticed a jet of water squirting into the sky. "Is that a whale?" she asked.

"It sure is," said Ted, steering the boat toward the water jet. "The whale is spouting water through its blowhole. That's the hole that the whale breathes through."

Jon had the video camera ready. The whale went below the water as the boat came up beside it. "He's gone," Jon cried.

"He'll be back," Sue told him. "He has to come up to breathe. Whales need to breathe air."

“Here’s what we’ll do when the whale comes up again. We’ll use a long pole and try to stick this video camera on the whale. The camera records sound, too,” Ted said. “People who do animal research call it a critter cam. This one is made to work under the water. It sticks onto the whale with **suction cups**.”

“Ted will steer the boat as close as he can and I’ll use this pole to put the critter cam on the whale,” Sue told them.

She showed them the critter cam. The **suction cups** were large. “The whale will hardly feel it,” Sue said.

The whale came above the water again. Sue got ready to attach the critter cam.

Liz grabbed the video camera. She leaned out over the side of the boat and began to film.

"It's on!" Sue told Ted as she stuck the critter cam onto the whale. Suddenly, the whale moved too close to the boat. The huge creature bumped against the boat. The whole boat rocked.

The video camera flew out of Liz's hands. "Oh, no!" she cried.

The camera flew up into the air. Jon and Liz reached up, hoping to catch it, but it was too far over the water. Just as the camera was about to fall into the sea, a fishing net swooped beneath it.

"That was close," said Mrs. Scott.

Jon and Liz nodded and smiled. "It sure was. Thanks, Mom," Liz said.

Chapter 5

A Video Surprise

By Monday, Liz and Jon were home. They were able to view their video on their TV.

They had seen three whales on the whale-watching trip. One of them had slapped a fin on the water and splashed them all, spraying drops of water on the lens.

"The day turned out to be fun for us. But I wish the video could have shown the whales under water," Jon said.

"I wish we could have heard the whales singing," said Liz.

"I wish the sound could be better," added Jon. "There's a lot of talking off screen."

Mr. Scott came in. He had heard the twins talking. "I have something that might help make your video better," he told them.

Jon and Liz ran to him. "What have you got?" Jon asked.

Mr. Scott loaded a video disc into the DVD player. It showed a humpback whale under water. It was calling out in its strange, amazing voice. Another huge humpback swam right past it.

"It looks like these two are friendly," Liz said.

"Maybe one of them is giving the other directions!" Jon added.

“Ted and Sue made this copy of their video for you,” Mr. Scott told them. “They thought you might like to add it to your school video.”

“This would make our video really amazing,” Jon said.

“I can help you edit their video so it works with your video,” Mr. Scott said. “Let’s get to work!”

Jon and Liz worked on the video all evening with their father. The next day, the twins sent the video in an e-mail to their friends back home.

On Thursday, Jon and Liz got an e-mail from their friends. A video came in the e-mail. It showed all the students in the school in the lunchroom. The students had just finished watching the whale video. Everyone clapped for the twins. Then they began making very strange noises.

"What are they doing?" Jon asked.

At first, Liz didn't know either. Then she understood. "I think they're making whale sounds," she said.

Jon and Liz joined in, making whale noises of their own. It felt like they were right there at their old school with their old friends. Then everyone in the lunchroom faced the camera and spoke together. They said, "That was whale talk for 'Thanks and come home soon!' "

"Whenever you miss home, you can play this video," Mrs. Scott told the twins.

That was just what they did.

Glossary

announced made it known that something is going to happen

fog a blanket of tiny water droplets that float over land or water

migrating traveling from one place or climate to another, usually on a regular schedule for feeding or breeding

research careful study of a subject in order to learn something new

suction cups bendable material that will stick when pressed onto a surface

university a school of higher learning; the next level of school after high school